D1106466

582   Edwards, Joan   c.1

Caring for trees on
city streets

SUBJECT TO LATE FINE

DATE			
FEB 24 78			
MAR 1 0 78			
OCT 29 82			
NOV 4 '8			
MAY 1 6			
DEC 0 8			
OCT 1 8 '07			

THE LIBRARY
CHILDREN'S LITERATURE COLLECTION
HUMBOLDT STATE UNIVERSITY
ARCATA, CALIFORNIA 95521

© THE BAKER & TAYLOR CO.

Caring for
TREES
on City Streets

Caring for TREES on City Streets

JOAN EDWARDS

for The Environmental Action Coalition

CHARLES SCRIBNER'S SONS NEW YORK

To the Bedford-Stuyvesant Neighborhood Tree Corps,
who first taught me about city trees.

ACKNOWLEDGMENTS

The Author and Publisher gratefully acknowledge the following for permission
to reproduce photographic material:

F. A. Bartlett Tree Expert Company, 33, 34, 37–39, 41 *(bottom)*; Brooklyn Union
Gas Company, 49–51; H. H. Lyon, Plant Pathology Dept., Cornell University, 41
(top), 42 *(top)*; Magnolia Tree Earth Center, 18, 35 *(top)*, 59; Len Maniace, 9
(bottom), 14 *(top)*, 15, 23, 28, 32, 35 *(bottom)*, 48 *(top)*, 52, 56, 58; Vi Matherson,
2, 7, 8, 9 *(top)*, 10–13, 14 *(bottom)*, 16, 17, 19, 20–22, 24, 25–27, 29–31, 36, 42
(bottom), 43–47, 48 *(bottom)*, 54, 57; Barry Spector, 60, 61.

Copyright © 1975 Environmental Action Coalition, Inc.
Copyright © 1973 Environmental Action Coalition, Inc.

This book published simultaneously in the
United States of America and in Canada—
Copyright under the Berne Convention
All rights reserved. No part of this book
may be reproduced in any form without the
permission of Charles Scribner's Sons.

1 3 5 7 9 11 13 15 17 19 MD/C 20 18 16 14 12 10 8 6 4 2

Printed in the United States of America
Library of Congress Catalog Card Number 75-16782
ISBN 0-684-144352

582
c.1

THE LIBRARY
CHILDREN'S LITERATURE COLLECTION
HUMBOLDT STATE UNIVERSITY
ARCATA, CALIFORNIA 95521

CONTENTS

1 Trees in the Life of a City 7

2 Street Tree Survival in a Concrete Environment 13

3 City Street Trees Need Your Help 23

4 Some Tree Problems Need Expert Help 33

5 Selecting City Street Trees 44

6 Some City Street Tree Favorites 49

7 Planting a City Street Tree 52

8 Adopt a Street Tree 58

9 Learn More by Yourself 60

For Further Reading 63

Index 64

1
Trees in the Life of a City

TREES ARE NICE TO LIVE WITH

People seem to remember cities filled with trees. In fact, some cities are famous for their beautiful parks and tree-lined avenues.

Trees are alive and moving against the still, unchanging buildings of a city. Their leaves and blossoms add color to the city. They soften the harsh outlines of cement, metal and glass. They change shape and color as the seasons change.

The shapes, colors and fragrances of trees are pleasant to live with. Their rustling leaves can make even a busy city street seem more peaceful. Trees can change cold, unfriendly places into inviting neighborhoods where people sit and chat on shady steps.

Street trees bring some peace and beauty to these busy midtown streets.

Trees are like hotels for many living things. They provide food and shelter for all kinds of birds and other animals. They share berries, nuts and seeds with birds and small animals. Birds, squirrels and insects use their branches, trunks, roots and leaves for homes.

TREES ARE OXYGEN PRODUCERS

We all need oxygen to live. We breathe in oxygen from the air and breathe out a gas called carbon dioxide. But where does all this oxygen come from? Why hasn't it been used up by now? The answer is that trees and other green plants put oxygen into the air. They take carbon dioxide out of the air when they make their food, and in the process they put oxygen back into the air.

Trees help supply the oxygen we need to breathe.

TREES ARE NATURE'S AIR-CONDITIONERS

In the summer the sun's direct rays are very strong. Concrete buildings and streets reflect this hot summer sun. But trees can help us escape the city heat on a hot summer day.

Trees shade us from the sun better than any sombrero. But that's not the only way they keep us cool. Trees also act like air-conditioners in the heat. The roots of trees send water from the soil to the leaves. Water in the leaves evaporates in the hot weather. This evaporated water helps to keep the air around a tree moist and cool.

Children playing in a concrete schoolyard are kept cool and comfortable by the shade trees lining this street.

Big trees with lots of leaves will evaporate more water than little trees with few leaves. A big elm tree on a hot summer day might give off 7 tons of water. It would make as much cool air as 10 room air-conditioners that are running for 20 hours.

Cool air is heavier than hot air. The cooler air under a shady tree sinks to the ground. It pushes up the warmer air. All this movement of air causes a breeze. Breezes make you more comfortable on a hot summer day.

Not long ago trees were the only air-conditioners we had. People planted trees to shade

Cars parked on city streets in summer can get very hot and stuffy. Trees in parking areas protect cars from the hot summer sun.

homes, playgrounds and park benches. Today many beautiful and cooling trees are torn down when homes, apartment buildings and office buildings are constructed. The hot sun then pours in unshaded windows. Often the windows of tall buildings can't even be opened to catch cooling breezes.

Air-conditioners are put in to cool these new buildings. These machines are replacing nature's air-conditioners. But they are also consuming precious energy and polluting our air. Trees use energy from the sun to cool us. And they cool us without polluting the air.

TREES HELP FIGHT POLLUTION

City air is dirty, smelly air. All the cars, trucks, busses, factories and incinerators in a city help to make it this way.

The leaves of trees help protect us from the dirt and gasses

Every day cars on busy streets give off harmful gasses, while factories and incinerators put dirt and more gasses into the air. More trees are needed on city streets to clean the air we breathe.

these things put in the air. Leaves have tiny hairs that catch dust and dirt from the air. When it rains, the dirt is washed off the leaves and returned to the ground.

Leaves also take some harmful gasses out of the air. Carbon dioxide is one of these gasses. We breathe out carbon dioxide after we take in oxygen from the air. Fuels also give off carbon dioxide when they are burned. Too much carbon dioxide in the air can harm our environment.

But trees help take this carbon dioxide out of the air. Leaves use it when they make food for the tree. Taking carbon dioxide out of the air isn't easy. Some experts say it takes 78 trees to remove the carbon dioxide that each person puts into the air each day when he breathes and uses fuel-burning machines.

Each spring new leaves appear on the tree to continue the

The leaves of trees help protect people from the dirt and gasses found in city air.

11

tree's pollution-fighting work. And remember that trees also return fresh oxygen into the air each day.

Trees can help fight noise pollution too. You can escape many city noises when you go to a big city park with lots of trees. A tree-lined street is quieter than a street with no trees. The trees seem to soak up noises —just like a sponge soaks up water!

Superhighways are noisy places. Trees and shrubs planted close together along highways act like a barrier to the sound waves, so that people who live near the highways will not be bothered by noisy cars and trucks.

Trees help muffle noisy city sounds, making a walk in the park (above) or a ride in a horse-drawn carriage a more enjoyable experience.

2
Street Tree
Survival
in a Concrete
Environment

Many trees on city streets are fighting for their lives. They have a hard time getting the air, water, food and sunlight they need to live. And each day some new enemy attacks and injures them.

Many street trees lose this struggle to survive. The average tree in a New York City park lives 50 to 75 years. Trees in the suburbs live longer. But a tree on New York City's streets, for example, will probably live only 10 to 40 years. And the trees with the shortest lives are on the busiest streets.

Soil is important in the life of a tree. Tree roots need room to spread out and grow. Roots get much of a tree's water, air and food from the soil. Soft, spongy soil rich in minerals helps trees grow strong and healthy.

Surrounded by concrete, street trees often have no room to grow.

In the forest, dead plants and animals decay and become part of the soil. This plant and animal matter in the soil is called *humus*. The soft and spongy humus lets air and water get to tree roots. The dead leaves covering the soil keep roots warm in winter and prevent moisture from escaping in summer. And the roots are fed constantly by decaying plant and animal matter.

The soil around city street trees doesn't contain this humus. Instead of humus, city street trees are surrounded by hard, packed soil and great slabs of concrete that strangle their roots and prevent them from growing.

Let's look more closely at some of the problems city street trees face.

Tightly packed soil around the base of a street tree prevents air from reaching its roots, sometimes causing the roots to suffocate.

TREE ROOTS NEED AIR

Roots need air to breathe just as much as other parts of a tree. They take in air from tiny openings in the soil. But street tree roots can have a hard time getting the air they need. This is because the soil around the base of a street tree is often packed down very tightly. People walk over the tree pit and pile garbage cans on it. Construction workers dump lumber, sand and other materials on it. These things cover and pack the soil down so much that air can't reach the roots.

Tree roots can suffocate under all this packed soil and the concrete that surrounds the tree. Sometimes harmful gasses and chemicals also develop in the packed, airless soil.

Unsightly litter packs down soil and keeps water from reaching tree roots.

ROOTS NEED WATER

Trees can get thirsty in a city. Hard, packed soil also prevents water from soaking down to the roots. When water stays at the top of the soil, it evaporates more quickly. Roots have to grow up instead of down to find water. And water sitting on the surface of the soil also cuts off air from the roots.

15

Enclosed by concrete and bricks, tree roots have trouble getting the water they need to survive.

Sometimes water has trouble even reaching the soil. Look up at a tree. Branches of a tree act like an umbrella. That's why you sometimes stand under a tree if you are caught in the rain. Water splashes off the leaves onto the ground. But if the branches go out over the sidewalk, the water splashes onto cement. It can't get into the soil and down to the roots.

Cement can also make water evaporate from the soil more quickly. Sometimes the cement around a tree acts like an oven and holds in the summer heat. This extra heat evaporates water that thirsty trees need. Tree roots can bake in this heat. Some street trees get burned very badly this way in the summer.

ROOTS NEED MINERALS FROM THE SOIL

In order to grow, trees must take many minerals from the soil. These minerals come from the tiny particles of rock and decaying matter that make up the soil. First, rainwater dissolves the minerals. Then tree roots absorb the minerals and water. The water and minerals move up the tree trunk to the leaves.

Each year tree roots absorb more and more minerals from the soil. But these minerals are often not replaced. In the forest, decaying plants and animals return minerals to the soil. But soil under a city street tree gets poorer each year. It has no way of replacing the minerals that trees use up.

Weeds and other plants can compete with street trees for precious minerals in the soil.

If trees cannot take minerals out of the soil, they will not be able to make food for themselves. They will get weaker and weaker. Finally decay and insects will enter the tree.

TREES NEED SUNLIGHT

Green leaves use minerals carried up from the soil to make food for the tree. They also use heat and light from the sun and carbon dioxide from the air. This food-making process is called *photosynthesis*.

But tall buildings can block the sunlight from a tree. Sometimes trees grow in funny directions, instead of straight up, because they are trying to reach sunlight that they need for photosynthesis.

City trees often grow crooked in their effort to reach the sunlight.

TREES NEED PROTECTION FROM GIRDLING

After leaves make food during photosynthesis, water carries food down to the rest of the tree. The food moves down the tree in a passageway close to the bark, called the *phloem*.

Sometimes something cuts off this passageway, and prevents the movement of food through the tree. A wire tied around a tree trunk might cut into the bark too tightly. Roots trying to find water might hit concrete or soil that is packed too hard and move back toward the tree. When such roots cross over the trunk or other roots, they strangle all or part of the tree.

When anything cuts through the phloem in this way it is called *girdling*.

When this tree was first planted, supporting wires helped hold the tree firmly in the ground. As the trunk got wider, the wires began to cut into the bark. Here the wires are being removed before they cut through the phloem.

TREES NEED PROTECTION FROM INJURIES

Girdling isn't the only way a tree can be injured. Tree roots can go very far in their search for food and water. Sometimes these roots are cut when roads, buildings, sewer lines or water pipes are being built or repaired. Then the rest of the roots have difficulty supplying the tree with enough food and water.

Bark is often damaged by careless people. Initials are carved in bark. Cars bump into trees while being parked. Signs are nailed onto tree trunks.

You must remember that a tree is alive. Bark protects a tree just like your skin protects you. When you cut into a tree, you are wounding it. Insects and disease can then enter the tree through the open wound.

Cars, vandalism and construction work injure or kill city street trees daily.

TREES NEED PROTECTION FROM DOGS

People aren't a tree's only enemies. Animals can do great damage to a tree.

Years ago, horses were a street tree's greatest enemy. People would hook their horse chains around trees when they stopped for a visit or to make deliveries. The horses loved to chew on the tree bark. Then decay would enter the tree through the damaged bark. Many trees died because of horses chewing on their bark.

Today dogs have replaced horses as the street tree's enemy. People often let their dogs use trees and the area around them as toilets. This hurts the tree by burning its bark and exposed roots and coating the pores of the tree. Poisons from dog droppings and urine can soak through the soil to the roots.

TREES NEED PROTECTION FROM HARMFUL CHEMICALS

When it snows, salt is often put on city streets to melt the snow. Then cars splash water with salt in it on street trees and the soil around them. People sprinkle salt on sidewalks to melt snow. The melting snow and salt go into the soil around the trees. All this dissolved salt can badly damage the tree trunk and roots.

Remember that a tree's tiny feeder roots are close to the soil's surface.

Salt isn't the only harmful chemical washed into the soil around street trees. Tree roots are also damaged by weed killers, gasoline, motor oil, kerosene, detergents and other chemicals carelessly spilled in tree pits.

TREES NEED PROTECTION FROM AIR POLLUTION

You know that trees can take some pollution gasses out of the air. But too much air pollution can make trees sick. Some trees are stronger than others, but trees can be hurt by polluted air just like people are. In fact, trees and other plant life can act like "pollution detectives." We can tell how serious air pollution is getting by looking at what it does to trees, bushes and flowers in our cities.

Leaves use sunlight when they make food for a tree. Polluted air can contain many tiny particles of dirt or soot. These particles fall to the earth, covering everything including the leaves of street trees. Too much soot on leaves can block out the sun and prevent photosynthesis.

Smoke in the air can also contain chemicals that damage leaves. These chemicals can also harm the tree in another way. Soil contains millions of tiny plants called bacteria. The bacteria helps to change minerals so that water can dissolve them for roots to use. Polluting gasses can kill some of these helpful bacteria.

There is a limit to the amount of air pollution street trees can tolerate. Even very hardy trees can be weakened by the constant pollution given off by factories, cars and busses.

21

TREES NEED PROTECTION FROM LOW TEMPERATURES

Very low temperatures and sudden drops in temperature can harm trees in two ways. They can cause cracks and other injuries on trunks. They can also damage branches and roots. Roots are especially injured when there is no snow on the ground in very cold weather. Snow acts like a blanket for the roots. In forests, the covering of dead leaves and twigs also helps keep tree roots warm. But the bare soil around street trees can't protect roots in cold weather.

TREES NEED PROTECTION FROM INSECTS AND DISEASES

Though not all insects are harmful to trees, some can weaken a tree by damaging its bark. And sometimes insects carry diseases from one tree to another.

Tree diseases can spread quickly along city streets. One reason is that often only a few kinds of trees are planted in a neighborhood. When one tree is infected, the disease quickly spreads to other trees in the same family, or *species.* If a greater variety of trees are planted, more trees will survive when one species becomes infected.

The damage caused by storms, cars, lawnmowers, nails and other objects is another reason tree diseases spread quickly—insects and diseases quickly enter these open, rotting wounds.

This tree, along with hundreds of others in the same community, was damaged by a winter storm.

3
City
Street Trees
Need
Your Help

Street trees need people as much as people need trees. They must be taken care of regularly, just like teeth or cars. But city workers are often too busy to give trees all the care they need.

You can help. You can protect trees from injury. You can help them get the things they need to live. And you can let tree experts know when trees are badly injured or diseased.

Look at the trees on your block. Ask yourself some questions. Is the tree getting enough water? Is it having trouble breathing? Can the roots get enough minerals from the soil? Is the bark injured? Do the leaves look green and healthy? Is there enough sunlight for the tree?

Now try the tree care suggestions in this chapter. You will need some equipment:

large pail   tree mulch
small garden trowel   work gloves
and hand rake   litter bag

GARBAGE AND TREES DON'T MIX

It's a shame to let ugly garbage ruin our enjoyment of lovely street trees. Litter also packs the soil down and prevents it from getting air and water.

Don't litter. Clean up the litter that people throw on the ground under trees. Remind shopkeepers and neighbors not to pile garbage cans around street trees.

Cleaning up littered tree pits is the first step in street tree care.

This screen makes it easier to clean up after people who think tree containers are garbage pails.

KEEP THE SOIL LOOSE

Cultivating, or digging up the soil around a tree, is one of the most important things you can do to keep street trees healthy.

Remember that loose soil helps water get down to the roots. It also allows air to circulate and get to the roots. Remember too that girdling roots occur more often in packed soils.

Soil should be cultivated year-round. In the summer, trees especially need the additional water that loose soil can help drain down to the roots. And in the winter, the air circulating in loose soil helps protect roots from low temperatures.

Use a small hand rake or trowel to dig up and loosen the top 2 to 3 inches of soil. *Be careful.* The tree's feeder roots are near the surface. Going down deeper might damage these roots.

You should also weed the area around each tree. Unattractive weeds can compete with trees for the scarce water, nutrients and air in the soil.

Cultivate the soil as often as necessary to prevent it from packing.

PUT MULCH ON THE SOIL

Since soil around street trees does not have a protective cover of decaying material, you must supply a cover for the soil. Spreading a cover of loose materials over soil is called *mulching.*

Mulch helps the tree in many ways. When mulch decays, it puts organic material back in the soil. This builds up the soil and makes it richer. Air can circulate easily through the loose pieces of mulch. And mulch helps prevent weeds from growing.

Wood chips are a good street tree mulch because they don't blow away and litter streets on windy days.

Mulch helps keep the ground warmer in winter and cooler in summer. In winter, it acts like a blanket and prevents the roots from freezing. In summer, it conserves water in the soil.

You can use a mulch made of peat moss, straw or wood chips. Leaves or sawdust might fly away and litter the streets. But they could be mixed in with whatever mulch you use.

During the winter the wood chips will slowly decay and return minerals to the soil.

Another good mulch is manure mulch. This will help feed the soil and protect it. But be very careful. Be sure the manure is well rotted. If it is not rotted enough, it could burn the roots of a tree. Ask a garden supply store for advice.

Cover the ground under the tree with 2 to 3 inches of mulch. Add new mulch as the old mulch rots or is blown away.

Mulch can be bought at garden supply stores. Try to buy it in large bags and shop around for a good price. It will probably be more expensive downtown than in the suburbs. Ask the parks department, horticultural society or garden club for advice about buying and using mulch in your area.

WATER THE SOIL AROUND STREET TREES

Water is another basic need that you can help supply to street trees.

Trees need watering year-round, but they need more water in summer. This is when leaves are most active making food for the tree. It is also when the hot sun and surrounding concrete are baking the soil and causing water to evaporate.

During very dry periods, trees should receive about 6 pails of water twice a week. This should be done at the end of the day, when the sun is low in the sky or after sunset.

You must always be careful not to drown trees. Remember that water will not drain well in packed and poor soils. This is why you should only water trees *after* the soil has been cultivated.

Do not allow the water to puddle on the top of the soil. Pour water slowly on the soil with a pail. If you use a hose, be careful to let it run very slowly into the tree pit. Stop as soon as water starts to puddle at the top.

Remember that rain does not always reach tree roots because of surrounding concrete. Trees need your help to get the water they need.

WASH AWAY SALT

You can protect a tree from the salt that is put on sidewalks and streets to melt snow. Take buckets of water and throw the water at the soil under the tree. This will wash the salt onto the street.

Don't use salt to melt the sidewalk in front of your home. Calcium chloride is better than salt. But even calcium chloride can hurt trees. Sand or sawdust is the best thing to use for melting snow or ice.

KEEP DOGS AWAY FROM STREET TREES

Don't let dogs use trees as toilets. Explain to dog owners that the bark and roots of trees are injured this way. Show them sections of dead or injured bark at the base of trees. Ask them to bring their dogs to the curb.

Some block associations put up signs on their street to remind people about this problem. One sign used in New York City says:

DOGS DON'T DISTURB
IF LED TO THE CURB.

Signs like this help remind dog owners to keep their animals away from street trees. You can make up your own signs—but remember not to tack or nail them to the tree.

SAVE A TREE

CURB YOUR DOG!
© 1974 Sign

PROTECT TREES—THEY'RE YOUR FRIENDS

Tell everyone how important healthy trees are to people. Ask them to stop doing things that harm trees. And try to get friends and neighbors to care for street trees also.

Don't let people wound trees by breaking branches or carving on them. Don't let them pour oil, gasoline, detergents or other harmful chemicals around the tree. Keep an eye out for trees that have garbage or construction materials piled around them.

Tree guards come in all shapes and sizes. The agencies listed on page 53 can suggest types of guards and places to buy them. Or you can save money and make your own.

Publicize tree problems and solutions. Put up signs in the neighborhood. (But don't tack or nail them onto trees.) Print flyers and pass them out.

Perhaps your class or youth group can make simple fences to put around trees so dogs, cars, lawnmowers and other things will have a harder time getting to trees.

Or try to get the people on your block to help you raise money for a more expensive tree guard. The best kind is one that can go up high around a tree.

These young people are making a tree guard as part of a class project on city tree care.

4
Some Tree Problems Need Expert Help

Trees often have problems that only an expert can solve. Let's look at some things tree experts do when caring for street trees. Some of these activities can also be done by an amateur who knows a lot about trees. But expert advice and help is always needed.

PRUNING
Often disease, dense shade, storms or other injuries can cause the ends of branches to die. All injured or dead wood should be cut off to prevent insects and diseases from entering the rest of the

tree. When parts of a tree are cut off in a special way, we call it *pruning*.

Pruning can be done for many reasons. Sometimes little shoots grow out of the trunk or come up out of the ground near the base of the tree. These ugly "sucker growths" use up precious water and food that the tree needs to live. So they are often pruned.

Branches might be removed if they could hurt themselves or others. Branches hanging out over the street could interfere with traffic or fall on people during a storm. Branches rubbing together might damage each other.

Tree experts use a crane to remove a dead tree from overhead wires (top left). After trees are pruned, the branches are fed into a machine which makes wood chips (left).

Here an entire tree fell over, causing severe damage. Dead branches of standing trees can also fall and do great harm, if not pruned properly.

A youngster receives instruction in proper pruning methods during an after-school program of the Bedford-Stuyvesant Neighborhood Tree Corps in New York City. He will be trained to prune very small branches and sucker growths under supervision.

Roots sometimes have trouble getting all the water and minerals a tree needs. If some of the top branches are cut off, the roots won't have to feed so much of the tree.

Pruning a tree isn't easy. In fact, some people think only an expert should prune a tree. Pruners use very special methods and tools. If a branch is not cut properly, part of the bark will be torn off the tree. Then disease and insects will enter the new tear. Special cuts after pruning also help scar tissue form more quickly.

Large branches are especially hard to prune correctly. But many people can learn how to prune tiny branches and sucker growths.

You can also watch out for trees that need pruning. Then call the parks department and let them know.

This young worker is pruning an injured branch to prevent insects and diseases from entering the rest of the tree.

PAINTING WOUNDS

Even carefully pruned trees have an open wound where the branch was cut off. All pruning cuts and other bark wounds must be painted with a special tree paint mixture. This covering will help keep disease out of the tree while the wound heals.

Pruners will paint the cuts they make. But you can help protect other injured trees. Special mixtures for painting tree wounds can be bought at a garden supply store. You can easily paint the mixture on bark injuries caused by cars or other objects.

An expert's helper paints the damaged bark with a special paint to protect it from diseases and insects.

REPAIRING CAVITIES

If a tree injury is not treated, decay can continue to spread and spread through the tree. Eventually there may be a very large hole where once there was only a tiny cut.

When decaying holes, or cavities, in tree trunks get too big they need special care. First the tree expert will remove as much dead and diseased wood as possible. Then he will cut the outside of the hole in a special way so that scar tissue will form quickly. This is the same kind of cut he makes when he prunes a tree.

A tree expert is cleaning decay out of a cavity.

This cavity has been cleaned and is ready for filling.

A tree expert has just filled this cavity.

This cavity, treated 7 years ago by a tree expert, has completely healed over. The tree's own scar tissue, the callus, covers the old wound.

If the hole is very large, the tree trunk will be weakened. It might not be able to support the weight of heavy branches or it might split open during a storm or fall over and injure someone. The tree expert can screw metal rods into the tree to make it stronger and leave the hole open. Or sometimes he will fill the hole with plastic, cement or some other mixture to strengthen the tree.

FERTILIZING

You now know how important soil is in the life of a tree. You also know that city trees often struggle to survive in very poor soil. One cause of poor soil is the lack of certain minerals. But minerals missing from poor soil can be replaced with a manufactured plant food—*fertilizer*. Fertilizer contains the minerals trees need to grow strong and healthy. It is usually added to the soil around the tree.

Remember that minerals are just the raw material for tree food. The tree still feeds itself in the same way. First water dissolves the fertilizer. Then the tree roots absorb the water and minerals.

Injections such as this are sometimes used for research on tree needs. Necessary minerals can also be injected into trees.

Water carries the dissolved minerals to the leaves where they manufacture food for the whole tree.

Tree feeding should only be done by someone who knows a lot about trees because there are many different kinds of fertilizers and many ways to feed a tree. Trees should usually be fed at certain times of the year. The fertilizer should be placed in special areas. Here are some of the things people who fertilize trees must know.

The three minerals trees need the most are nitrogen, phosphorus and potassium. They are also the minerals that are most often missing from the soil. Nitrogen helps the tree produce healthy wood, twigs and green leaves. Phosphorus is needed to help roots grow. Potassium helps trees manufacture the sugar and starches they need to be strong and healthy.

All tree fertilizers contain nitrogen, phosphorus and potassium. But they don't all contain the same amount of these minerals. The label on a bag, can or bottle of fertilizer contains three numbers, such as 6-8-6, 10-8-6, etc. The first number tells the percentage of nitrogen, the second tells the percentage of phosphorus and the third tells the percentage of potassium. Many fertilizers also contain small amounts of other minerals also needed by trees.

Trees are usually fertilized in late fall or early spring. While there are several ways to fertilize a tree, the *punch-bar* method is the most popular way to add fertilizer to the soil. Holes are punched in the soil around the tree. The holes are only 12 to 18 inches deep because a tree's feeder roots are near the surface. The holes are punched in the area under the outer branches, where most feeder roots grow. The holes are filled with fertilizer and then covered with soil. They are then watered to help dissolve the minerals. Remember that roots absorb minerals dissolved in water.

The "For Further Reading" section at the back of the book lists some places to learn more about fertilizing trees.

Galls on Norway Maple.

YOU CAN HELP THE EXPERTS OUT

It isn't easy to prune, fertilize or fill cavities in street trees. But you can help report diseased and damaged trees to the parks department so they can send a tree expert out to care for the tree. By catching a problem early, you might be able to save a tree that would have died.

Study trees in your neighborhood. Look for signs that trees may be suffering from air pollution, damaging insects, lack of food and other problems. You might not be able to tell exactly what is harming the tree. But there are certain signals that show a tree is having problems. Some signals are listed on the following pages.

Tree experts depend on scientific work in the laboratory for increased knowledge of trees and tree care.

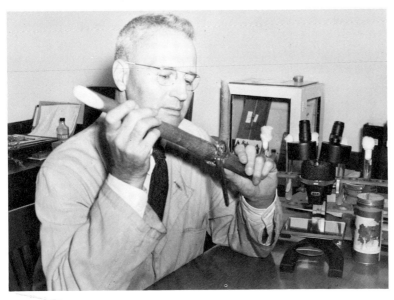

Black leaf spot of Elm tree.   Disease and insect problems endanger many city street trees. They must be diagnosed and treated by experts, although you can learn to recognize some of the symptoms below. Busy city workers can use your help in locating trees that require treatment.

LEAF SYMPTOMS

small yellow leaves

parts of the leaf shriveled or turned under or upward

brown, dead areas that look like a net on a green leaf

any unusual markings or change in color on the leaf

leaves drying out and falling off the tree before autumn

BRANCHES OR TWIGS

many dead twigs

dead or broken branches

branches rubbing together

many suckers growing out of the base of the tree

These sucker growths are using up precious water and minerals that the tree needs. They should be pruned.

TRUNK

    damaged trunk

    a smelly, ugly liquid dripping from wounds in the bark or wood

ROOTS

    girdling caused by some tree roots crossing over the trunk or other roots on the surface

    a large swelling at the base of the trunk (often caused by girdling roots underground)

CROWN

    one group of branches has many more leaves than another group

A car bumped into this tree, scraping off its protective bark. If the wound is not treated with special pruning paint, insects and disease might enter the tree or it may begin to rot.

5
Selecting
City
Street Trees

If people all over the world closed their eyes this minute and thought about trees, they would all be imagining different trees. Trees are not all alike. Some trees need a lot of soil because they have big, sprawling roots. They grow best in the country where there is room for them to spread out. Some trees need lots of water. Willow trees do. They can't grow in the desert. But desert palms don't mind. They don't need a lot of water to live. There are all kinds of trees in the world because the environment is different in each place.

Some trees can adapt well to city life. Others cannot. Not all city environments are alike. Some cities have more air pollution. Others have harsher winters. So trees that grow well in one city might not grow well in another.

Attractive evergreens are often planted in containers on busy city streets. But evergreens do not adapt well to pollution from cars and busses and soon become sick or die from dirt and gasses in the air.

Trees that grow well in one neighborhood might even die many blocks away. For example, some neighborhoods have many skyscrapers that block out the sunlight. Other neighborhoods have smaller buildings with sunny sidewalks.

City environments can change. Some trees that grew well in a city years ago are dying today. People in Tokyo, Japan, are very worried about their beautiful Japanese Flowering Cherry trees. There used to be many of these trees in Tokyo. But now they are dying. There are more factories and cars in Tokyo now and the pollution from them is killing the cherry trees. Selecting a street tree is not a simple matter. The right tree must be matched up with the right environment. Here are some things to think about when deciding which trees belong on city streets.

WHY IS THIS TREE BEING PLANTED?
Is the tree wanted to protect homes, cars and people from the hot summer sun? If so, you will want a large shade tree. Do you want to attract birds to your street with this tree? Or do you and your neighbors want a pretty tree with flowers in the spring or bright colors in the autumn? If the tree is replacing one that has died, will the new one look well with the other trees on the street?

The red fruits of this Hawthorn tree stay on its branches all winter, giving a bit of color to a drab city street. On a less busy street, the berries will also attract birds.

Some branches have already been pruned from this tall tree to make room for the overhead wires. However, the wires are still cutting the bark as the tree grows.

HOW BIG SHOULD THE TREE BE?

Trees with wide, spreading roots near the surface cannot be planted in an area surrounded by concrete. Short trees with wide, spreading branches can interfere with traffic. And very tall, fast-growing trees can't be planted under overhead wires. Ginkgo trees, for example, are very slow-growing and are often preferred on busy city streets.

CAN THE TREE LIVE IN YOUR CITY'S CLIMATE AND WEATHER?

Some trees would die quickly in a harsh, cold climate. Trees needing a lot of water could not survive a hot, dry summer surrounded by concrete. Trees with shallow roots are easily blown over in a windy city. And trees on streets near the ocean must survive the salty ocean spray blown by winds.

WILL INSECTS AND DISEASE HARM THE TREE?

Remember that the bark of city street trees is often injured. Insects and disease can then enter this damaged bark. Trees that are easily infected by disease should not be planted on city streets.

IS THE TREE MESSY OR DANGEROUS?

Some trees are very messy. They shed seeds, fruit, blossoms, twigs, cones and bark, in addition to leaves.

These things litter our streets and sidewalks. Sometimes they can also make life very unpleasant for city dwellers. For example, the female ginkgo tree has a very smelly fruit that breaks when it falls on sidewalks. That is why only male ginkgo trees are planted in cities today. Trees with sharp thorns can injure adults and children walking and playing on city streets.

Street trees are best planted in strips of grass between the sidewalk and the street. Their roots have more room to spread out for food and water here than in tiny tree pits surrounded by cement.

City street trees must be super-trees. We expect them to be attractive and to improve our environment. We also expect them to be tough enough to survive on cement-covered, polluted city streets. City trees can live up to our expectations with a little help from us.

IS THE TREE STRONG ENOUGH TO SURVIVE ENVIRONMENTAL DAMAGE?

Remember all the problems city trees face. Only the strongest trees can be planted on city streets. They must be able to survive the air pollution, poor soil, bark injury, dogs and other environmental problems they will face in the city.

TREE EXPERTS ARE FINDING THE ANSWERS

It is not easy to find the right tree for a city street. But tree experts are doing a lot of research. They have found some trees that can adapt to a city environment. And they are learning how to grow new kinds of trees that can survive city life.

Tree experts know that the ginkgo tree survives very well on city streets. But ginkgoes are not a new type of tree. They were growing in prehistoric times and were brought here from Japan and China. The ginkgo tree in this photo is thriving in front of a skyscraper on a busy midtown street.

6
Some City Street Tree Favorites

Maple trees are easy to recognize by the shape of their leaves and their green winged seeds.

The Ailanthus tree, often called the Tree of Heaven, is a very hardy tree. Although usually not planted by city dwellers (it is regarded as a pest by many), it grows well all over the city—in yards, vacant lots and even in pavement cracks near buildings.

You can easily recognize the London Plane tree by its peeling yellowish brown bark. This fast-growing tree is very well adapted to city life. It can tolerate heat, lack of water, dust and poisonous gasses. But it has been planted so often in many cities that disease can strike whole blocks of trees.

The Catalpa has lovely white flowers and broad, heart-shaped leaves.

The floppy branches and lovely fan-like leaves of ginkgo trees make a nice contrast to tall, straight skyscrapers.

The pretty Linden is a hardy tree that gives lots of shade.

7
Planting
a City
Street Tree

These days many people are buying trees for their neighborhoods. They want more green on city streets. You know now that it takes a lot of study to decide which trees will grow best in each city and in each neighborhood. And it takes a lot of work to keep the trees you plant healthy.

But even after you decide on a particular tree, there are many questions to be answered. Trees cost money. Who will pay for these trees? Where will you buy them? Where will you plant them? You must get permission to plant the tree if it will be on city property. And who will do the work? If a tree is not planted properly, it could die. You must do a lot of research if you want to plant a tree.

There are many organizations and government agencies that will answer your questions about selecting, planting and caring for street trees. Ask for help from one of the following agencies or from one of the companies or organizations listed on page 63. You can get help in finding their addresses from the phone book, local library or government officials.

City Parks Department
Department of Highways
Department of Agriculture
State agricultural experiment station
State extension landscape specialist
County agricultural agent
Horticultural society
Garden club
Block association
Nursery

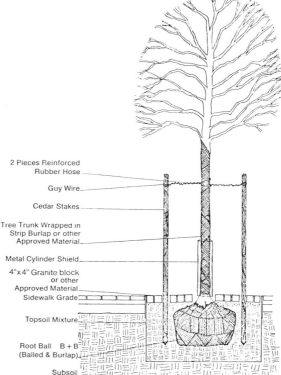

2 Pieces Reinforced Rubber Hose
Guy Wire
Cedar Stakes
Tree Trunk Wrapped in Strip Burlap or other Approved Material
Metal Cylinder Shield
4"x4" Granite block or other Approved Material
Sidewalk Grade
Topsoil Mixture
Root Ball   B + B (Balled & Burlap)
Subsoil

This illustration shows the preparation made by the New York City Parks Department when they plant a street tree.

GETTING PERMISSION

If you are going to plant the tree on private property, you probably only need the owner's permission. But if you want to plant the tree on city property, you must first find out what rules and regulations your city has about tree planting. Call the parks department and the highway department. Ask if you need a permit to plant a tree, and whether you can plant any kind of tree. Also ask if the city has a list of recommended street trees. Find out if the site has to be inspected by a city official. (You might be planning to plant a tree right over a water pipe or underground wire!) Ask if the tree must be planted by an expert. You might want to know if the city has a list of recommended nurseries that give guarantees for the trees they sell. You will also want to know if the money spent on the tree is tax-deductible.

WHO WILL PLANT THE TREE?

Once you find out the rules about planting street trees and decide which tree you want to buy, you must decide who will plant the tree. Some cities allow individuals and organizations to plant the tree themselves. However, tree planting is not easy. Many people feel that trees should be planted only by tree experts. These experts will prepare the hole for the new tree. They will make sure it has room to grow

This newly planted street tree is well supported by stakes and wires. It is protected from the sun by burlap and from dogs by the metal base.

and some soft, rich soil to grow in. If necessary, they will fix the ground so that water will drain down to all the roots. They can make sure the roots are not damaged in planting. They know how to support the tree while its roots are getting anchored and what to use to protect young trees from the hot sun and cold winter frost.

Large trees must always be planted by tree experts. Smaller trees are easier to plant. They also get used to their new environment more easily. If you do decide to plant the tree yourself, get help from someone who has planted trees before.

WHEN TO PLANT

Most trees should be planted in late fall or spring. The roots of many young trees freeze and die during the winter. If the winters are very cold in your city, it might be better to wait until spring. If the trees are planted in fall, mulch should be put on the ground to protect the roots from frost.

DIGGING THE HOLE

This is the most important step in planting a tree. The best tree will die when transplanted if its new home is not properly prepared.

The hole must be larger than the roots of the new tree so that the new roots will have room to grow. The soil must be examined. New roots need soft soil with lots of minerals so if the soil has too much sand or clay, it must be replaced with dark, soft, rich topsoil. The new tree's tender rootlets must be able to push easily into the soil as they begin to grow.

Trees can drown from too much water. Water may not drain properly at the site you selected. Gravel or sand must then be put at the bottom of the hole. This will keep water from standing around the tree's roots.

PLANTING THE TREE

The tree must be placed very gently and carefully in its new home. If the roots are damaged, they will not be able to feed and support the tree properly. The roots must be spread out so that they do not cross over each other and girdle the tree. When the soil is put back into the hole, the roots must be completely covered and the soil packed down gently but firmly.

AFTER PLANTING

The job is still not done when the tree is in and the soil replaced. Newly planted trees need a lot of help adjusting to their new home. The roots must grow and take hold of the soil. At first, they need help supplying food and water to the tree.

They must be watered thoroughly. If any roots were cut or damaged while planting, the top branches must be pruned. Remember that pruning makes it easier for roots to supply food and water to the rest of the tree. Stakes placed alongside the tree will help support it while the roots are growing.

The bark of young trees is easily burned by the hot sun and dried by winter winds. Wrapping burlap or a special type of paper around tree trunks will protect the bark from bad weather.

YOUNG TREES NEED EXTRA CARE

Young trees also need time to get used to their new home. Be sure to water young trees carefully the first two years after they are planted. Don't rip off the covering around the tree trunk for about two years. And check the wires supporting the tree. If they are girdling the tree trunk, call the parks department. Be sure to put mulch over the tender young roots in late fall so that they don't freeze in the frost.

CONTAINER TREES

Street trees are often planted in large containers placed on the sidewalk. These can be very attractive, but they are not always practical. Only certain smaller trees should be planted in containers. The roots of large trees cannot spread out in these containers. They wrap around each other and kill the tree.

These trees will someday outgrow their home in this attractive container.

8
Adopt a
Street Tree

This young man is hanging a sign that will let the community know he and his friends care for the trees on this street.

Adopt a tree near your home or school. Learn all about it. Study it. Water it when it is thirsty. Protect it from animals and people who don't care. Call the parks department if it is sick or damaged.

Get together with a group of friends and adopt trees on a whole block. Go out together regularly to care for street trees.

Take a "tree census" of your neighborhood. First map the streets near you. Then find out what kinds of trees are on these streets. Find out about their health and the condition of their soil. Record your findings and let others know what you've found out.

You will need some equipment for your tree census. Get several different magic markers, a sheet of poster board, pencil and paper, a ruler and a guide to city trees and leaves.

Start with one square block in your neighborhood. Bring along a tree guide and a pencil and paper. Make a map by marking out the outlines of the block on the paper and labeling each street.

Walk around the block and put a circle on the map to represent each tree you find. Label the circle with the name of the tree it represents.

Transfer the map and information to a large piece of poster board. Color code the trees. For example, color in all the circles representing London plane trees in red and ginkgo trees in orange.

Now you can tell at a glance just how many street trees your neighborhood contains, where they are located, which species have been planted and which species are missing.

A tree census can tell you a lot about the trees that surround you and their future needs. You might be surprised at some of your findings. You could make maps showing the condition of trees or the soil under the tree. You could map trees that have tree guards. You could mark trees that have a special history or are very old. You could make any kind of map you choose that tells people more about the street trees in your community.

Remember, city street trees are struggling to survive in a concrete environment. If you don't care about them, who will?

These young people belong to the Bedford-Stuyvesant Neighborhood Tree Corps, which has been caring for city street trees since 1971. Tree Corps members attend after-school classes year-round to learn the rudiments of gardening and care for the street trees in their community during the warm weather.

9
Learn More by Yourself

1. WATER DRAINS THROUGH CULTIVATED SOIL FASTER THAN PACKED SOIL

You will need:

pencil and paper

juice can with both ends removed

large can or pail of water

small garden rake or trowel

measuring cup

watch with second hand

See for yourself what a difference cultivating the soil makes. First take a pencil and stick it into various areas of the soil around a street tree. Find a place where the pencil will not go far into the soil.

Force the juice can part way into the compacted area of the soil. Pour water into the can. Write down how much water you poured and time how long it takes for the water to drain into the soil.

Dig up another area of the same tree pit. Cultivate the soil until it is nice and loose. Push the juice can the same distance into the cultivated soil. Pour the same amount of water into the can. Time how long it takes for the water to percolate into the soil.

Did both cans empty out at the same rate? What was the difference in time? Did the water in either can stay on top of the soil? Try this experiment in different kinds of soils.

2. LEAVES "TRANSPIRE," OR EVAPORATE, WATER ON A HOT, SUNNY DAY

You will need:

| plastic bag | tree with low branches or |
| string | houseplant |

See for yourself how much water "nature's air-conditioners" give off to cool the air.

Tie a small plastic bag around a few leaves hanging on a low tree branch. Leave it for a few hours on a hot, sunny, summer day. Then check to see if moisture has collected on the inside of the bag.

In the fall, leaves will soon seal off their stems and transpiration in tree leaves will stop. But trees are plants and all plants transpire. You could do this same experiment by placing the bag on a plant on a sunny windowsill.

These students are doing "bark rubbings," a fun way to learn more about different trees. They gently rub a soft crayon over the onion skin paper placed on the tree bark.

3. MINERALS DISSOLVED IN WATER RISE THROUGH PLANT STEMS

You will need:

    jar or glass   white carnation or daisy   scissors
    water   food coloring

See for yourself how plants absorb minerals dissolved in water and lift them up through the stem.

Put some water in the bottom of the glass. Add a lot of coloring. Clip off part of the flower stem at the bottom. Put the stem in the water and leave it overnight.

The next morning look at the flower. Is it still white?

FOR FURTHER READING

Burchardt, Nellie. *What Are We Going to Do, Michael?* New York: Franklin Watts, Inc., 1973. A story how a ten-year-old boy and his next-door neighbor save a rare magnolia tree from destruction by an urban renewal project.

Gallob, Edward. *City Leaves, City Trees.* New York: Charles Scribner's Sons, 1972. A good book to use for identification of city trees in the New England, Middle Atlantic, and North Central states. Large, clear photographs of each tree, its leaves, buds, and fruit.

Howell, Ruth. *A Crack in the Pavement.* New York: Atheneum Publishers, 1970. A book about the many living things which may be found in a large city. Many interesting photographs.

U.S. Department of Agriculture Forest Service. *A Tree Hurts, Too.* New York: Charles Scribner's Sons, 1975. A fully illustrated book that outlines what happens when decay develops in a living tree.

The following companies and organizations can also provide information about city trees:

American Association of
   Nurserymen, Inc.
835 Southern Building
Washington, D.C. 20005

American Horticultural Society
Mount Vernon, Virginia 22121

Bartlett Tree Experts
2770 Summer Street
Stamford, Connecticut 06905

Chevron Chemical Company
Public Relations
200 Bush Street
San Francisco, California 94120

Environmental Action Coalition
235 East 49th Street
New York, New York 10017

Magnolia Tree Earth Center of
   Bedford-Stuyvesant, Inc.
1512 Fulton Street
Brooklyn, New York 11216

National Audubon Society
930 Third Avenue
New York, New York 10017

The Parks Council
80 Central Park West
New York, New York 10023

INDEX

Ailanthus, 49
air pollution: damage to trees by, 21, 45, 48;
removal of by trees, 10–12

bark rubbings, 61
Bedford-Stuyvesant Neighborhood Tree Corps, 35, 59

calcium chloride, 30
carbon dioxide, 11
Catalpa, 50
cavities, 37, 38
census, 58–59
climate, 46
containers, 57
cooling properties, 9
cultivation, 25, 26

disease, 22, 33, 36–37, 47;
symptoms of, 42–43
dogs, 20, 30, 48

esthetic qualities, 7

feeding: by man, 26, 28, 38–40;
process in tree, 11, 17–18, 62;
punch bar method of, 40

Ginkgo, 46–48, 51, 59
girdling, 18, 19, 25, 43, 56, 57
guards, 31, 32

Hawthorn, 45
humus, 14

injuries, mechanical, 19, 36;
painting of, 36
insects, 19, 22, 33, 41, 47

Japanese Flowering Cherry, 45

lifespan, 13
Linden, 51
litter, 15, 24, 31, 47
London Plane, 50, 59

Maple, 49
mulching, 26, 27, 28, 57

nitrogen, 39
noise pollution, 12

oxygen, 8, 11, 12

phloem, 18
phosphorus, 39
photosynthesis, 17, 18, 21
planting, 52–57
pollution. See air pollution, noise pollution
potassium, 39, 40
pruning, 33–37, 42, 46

soil: chemicals in, 20, 30–31;
importance of, 13, 14, 15;
improvement of, 25–29, 38;
quality of, 14–16, 18, 22;
water drainage in, 15–16, 25, 29, 55–56, 60
sucker growths, 34, 35, 42, 43

transpiration, 9, 61

watering, 29, 57
weather: damage to trees by, 22, 29, 38, 46;
protection of trees from, 25, 27, 55, 57
weeding, 26
Willow, 44